Re:CONSIDERING

THE END OF THINKING?

Mark Stephens

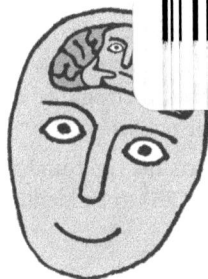

I0113874

a. Acorn
Press

Published by Acorn Press, an imprint of Bible Society Australia, in partnership with the Centre for Public Christianity.

ACN 127 775 973
GPO Box 4161
Sydney NSW 2001
Australia

www.publicchristianity.org

ISBN 9780647531303 (pbk)
ISBN 9780647531310 (ebk)

A catalogue record for this book is available from the National Library of Australia

Editor: Owen Salter
Cover and text design: John Healy

About the Centre for Public Christianity

What is the good life?
What does it mean to be human?
Where can I find meaning?
Who can I trust?

In sceptical and polarised times, the Centre for Public Christianity (CPX) seeks to engage the public with a clear, balanced, and surprising picture of the Christian faith. A not-for-profit media company, since 2007 CPX has been joining the dots between contemporary culture and the enduring story of Jesus in the articles, podcasts, books, documentaries, and other resources we produce.

We believe Christianity still has something vital to say about life's biggest questions. Find out more about our team and the work we do at www.publicchristianity.org or follow us on Facebook, Twitter, and Instagram.

CPX CENTRE
FOR
PUBLIC
CHRISTIANITY

About the author

Dr Mark Stephens is a Senior Research Fellow at the Centre for Public Christianity (CPX). He has a PhD in Ancient History from Macquarie University, and a Masters in Divinity from the Australian College of Theology. For 10 years Mark was lecturer at Excelsia College, teaching performing artists how to use their creativity to help audiences think deeply. Contrary to all rational thinking, Mark is a lifelong supporter of the Parramatta Eels rugby league team.

CONTENTS

INTRODUCTION:
ONE NIGHT IN TENNESSEE

In May 2003 I took my first and only trip to Memphis. It wasn't my choice.

To say that my wife has an affection for Elvis is like saying Gollum has an affection for rings. She adores everything about the man. Including his frozen-in-time, interior-decorating-disaster of a house. Otherwise known as Graceland.

Me? I was more interested in saving money for bigger cities. To that end, I had the brilliant idea of booking a hotel three miles out of downtown. I figured that even with the cost of cabs, we would still end up $15 to the good. $15, people. Frugality is my love language.

On our first evening we enjoyed dinner downtown and then took a cab home. In the dim light, I mistook a 20 for a 1, and paid my driver 26 bucks for a three-mile trip. I'm sure he was happy. I was inconsolable.

By the next evening I was still seething, frantically looking for an opportunity to make my money back. There was no Uber, no Lyft. By the time we needed the cab back to our hotel, I was desperate for a win.

So there I was, standing with my young wife out the front of a bus shelter, when a saviour approached.

He was a complete stranger, in crumpled leather jacket, dirty jeans, and missing most of his teeth. I already know what you're thinking – Mark, this is your driver.

'You want a ride?'

For some reason which eludes me, I replied: 'How much?'

'$7.'

'Pfft. I can get a cab for 6.'

'All right then, $5.'

Ladies and gentlemen, we have a deal.

As I shoved my bride into the back of a beaten-up Pontiac, I couldn't help noticing that the steering wheel was held on by gaffer tape. Our 'driver' then informed us it wasn't actually his car, and he needed to go borrow the keys. I didn't venture to ask if the owner knew his car was now a loaner.

For the next five minutes of my life, my wife gripped my hand tightly. It was her way of feeling safe. It was also a signal of what she intended to do to my throat once the car trip concluded.

What happened? Nothing.
Except I saved myself a buck.

What were you thinking?

Every time I tell this story to friends, the question is the same as my wife's on that night.

What were you thinking?

The simple answer is I wasn't thinking. Or at least I wasn't thinking well.

But perhaps the more interesting point is our assumption that people *should* be thinking. We expect people to do things for a good reason. We require of our decisions a thought process. The French philosopher René Descartes famously defined a human being as a 'thinking thing' (*res cogitans*). While dear old René was exaggerating, the mind plays a large role in much of our lives.

We're anxious about thought from the very beginning. Nearly every baby toy or iPhone app claims to be 'growing young minds'. This is usually just a convenient lie to conceal that Mum or Dad need some time out to avoid complete emotional collapse. But to assuage parental guilt we tell ourselves that the Paw Patrol Rescue Racer we just bought is helping our child become the next Einstein.

3

For many of us, the first two decades of life (and even a few more) will be mostly spent in formal education. Primary, secondary, tertiary – the centrality of our minds seems ever more emphatic. Modern Westerners live in what Peter Drucker has dubbed a 'knowledge economy', where people pay us for ideas and information.

And that's just our work life. In every sphere, being a grown-up seems to assume you can think for yourself. The German philosopher Immanuel Kant defined enlightenment as having the courage to use your own reason. We need to vote for politicians, choose which property to buy, commit to romantic partners, tell our kids what they should eat, assess our carbon footprint, and pick our religion.

Figure it out for yourself.

Make up your own mind.

It's your call.

We *expect* that people can think for themselves.

Yet the question 'What were you thinking?' highlights something else. We ask it when thinking appears to fail, when someone (most often ourselves) does something stupid, thoughtless, crazy, or irrational. It doesn't have to be an epic fail. 'Idiot brain' happens even in the little things. Mistakes were made. Something was missed. We could have thought more about that. I had the wrong idea.

And then we shrug our shoulders and move on. But should we be so blasé?

We expect people to be thinking.

We regularly fail.

For all the education we receive, most adults never *think* about their *thinking*. Like breathing or walking, thinking seems to be an assumed skill that, achieved once, rarely needs revisiting. I tore my Achilles tendon in 2019, and part of the rehab was staying off my left foot for six weeks. When the moon boot finally came off and my emaciated leg finally reconnected with earth, it felt for a brief moment like a return to childhood. Nobody wants to relearn how to walk. Few of us want to revisit how to think.

The point here isn't that any adult ever stops learning about new subjects, facts, or opinions. Gluten-free baking, bitcoin investment, systemic racism, climate change – the modern self is constantly stimulated by new ideas.

The point is, do we know *how* to think well about all this new information? Do we appreciate it when someone asks hard questions of our opinions? Do we care about finding truth, or just being seen to be right?

Perhaps the big underlying question here is what end we have in mind. Do we think only for ourselves, or do we also think for the good of others?

In the main, I am not speaking to those small areas of life where we've managed a passable level of expertise. If you're an oncologist, you'll probably know cancer. If you're a history teacher, I'm guessing you've got World War II mostly covered. If you're a civil engineer, there's no need to revisit introductory physics.

But our thought life goes well beyond our small domains of expertise. Even in your chosen profession you will have to think about so much more than what you are explicitly trained for. Accountants need to think about mental health. Nurses need to vote. Journalists need to consider the claims of a religion. We're always thinking. And we can all do it better.

This little book aims to help you think. It won't give you many answers, but it might help you ask better questions. However, the goal is a touch more ambitious than that. My larger aim is to help you become a better person who uses your thinking to serve other people.

There is nothing wildly innovative about my perspective. My take on thinking has been substantially formed and nurtured by my identity as a Christian believer. For all of its faults, it might come as a surprise that the Christian tradition has helped me understand and practise thinking with others in mind.

Thinking is a deeply human activity, and the way we go about it reveals much about our character. And thinking happens everywhere, not just in classroom or lecture hall. I'm aiming at the conversation in the cafe, the discussion in your boardroom, the late-night chat with your teenage daughter. Because *you* are always thinking. And that means we need to consider the 'you' who is doing the thinking.

1. A THOUSAND WAYS TO FALL

It is always simple to fall; there are an infinity of angles at which one falls, only one at which one stands.

G.K. Chesterton, *Orthodoxy*

Assuming for a moment that our thinking can be mistaken, it is helpful to get a sense of why we fail. Where does our thinking go wrong?

That all depends on who you ask. It turns out that thinking can be a complicated business, and there are a range of experts who can offer help. Here we are going to draw upon the wisdom of three different domains: philosophy, psychology, and statistics. Each offers a different insight into why we don't think well.

Philosophy

Let's start with philosophers. If you type the phrase 'great thinkers' into an online bookstore, there's a better than average chance a philosophy text will pop up. Indeed, the base definition of 'philosopher' is someone who *loves wisdom.*

Within philosophy, there are sub-disciplines specifically devoted to the art of thinking, such as epistemology. Epistemology is, let's be honest, a mouthful of a word. Sometimes it's more easily labelled the 'theory of knowledge'. Put simply, how can we reliably claim to 'know' something?

Like many topics in philosophy, at first this might strike us as making a simple thing complicated. But claiming knowledge *is* more complex than we first think. We casually make statements like 'climate change is real' or 'that person is corrupt', or even just the general claim 'I know what I saw.' We have all had conversations over coffee where someone tells us what they 'know' to be true. And at least some of the time we want to reply, 'How do you *know* that? I can see you *believe* it, but how do you *know* it?'

Philosophers press us to consider what justification or grounds we have to claim something as knowledge. Does the evidence of our senses always guide us to truth? Are our memories reliable? How do we weigh the value of other people's testimony? This is not the place to give you a philosophy lesson. The point here is simpler – you should have reasons for believing.

This matters in every part of life. It matters when your friend recommends an investment. It matters in staff meetings. It matters on your Facebook chat. It matters when a US president suggests injecting bleach. We are wise to seek reasons, justifications, and evidence before we move something from the hope column into the knowledge column.

We might have all sorts of beliefs. Some of them could even be true. But without justifications – we don't *know* much.

Even in the everyday, this is part of why our thinking fails us. We often do not feel the need to adequately support our claims.

We fire out opinions like we're playing unlimited paintball with friends. And then we get offended when people stop and ask us hard questions, daring to suggest we might need some better reasons.

Psychology

A second source for understanding how thinking goes wrong is psychology. As I said before, if you type 'great thinkers' into an online bookstore, you're likely to turn up a philosophy text. But over the last few decades, the real movers and shakers have been psychologists.

Psychologists unveil how our brains are highly motivated and easily biased. A great many experiments show that our minds are predisposed to process information in habitual ways, not all of which prioritise finding the truth.

The classic example is confirmation bias. Confirmation bias is the habit that, once we believe something to be true, we then shut our minds off from seriously considering alternatives. It's the mistaken idea that what we see must be all there is. What we forget is how we sift evidence selectively, because all we want is confirmation of what we already believe. Turns out being open-minded does not come easily. And the reason isn't because your evidence is unassailable and your arguments precise. The reason is us and our motivated brains. We prefer reinforcement over finding the truth.

The social psychologist Jonathan Haidt argues that intuitions come first and reasoning comes second. Our initial responses are pretty automatic, what we might call a gut-level reaction. And then our reasoning follows our gut, playing the role of an 'inner lawyer' who defends our intuition. It's not think and then respond. It's respond and then defend.

One of the chief ways our gut influences thinking is the feeling of repugnance. When a person or their viewpoint disgusts us, we find it impossible to think through the idea. Emotions forestall the possibility of thought. But here's the thing. In our polarised social-media-fuelled age, it seems easier to be disgusted by those who don't think like us. I don't just disagree with you; I'm repulsed by you.

Before we go too much further, it needs to be said that our mental biases can prove useful. The psychologist Daniel Kahneman talks about how 'thinking fast' involves mental shortcuts which work well enough, most of the time. Life is filled with so much information that we require thinking 'fast' just to get stuff done. You can't ponder every moment of your life. As I wake up, how certain am I that my shower really exists? How does eating my cereal contribute to global injustice? Do I perform a meticulous safety check on my car every time I drive it? Live your life pondering everything and you'll end up in the foetal position on your bed. Or watching Netflix. Which is roughly the same thing.

The problem is not that we think fast *sometimes*. That's necessary. The problem is when we *never* think slowly. As Erin Devers and Jason Runyan put it: 'Automatic thinking is what frees us up to think slowly and deliberately about certain matters. Deliberate thinking is a limited resource that needs to be used wisely.'

All of this means that if you are going to think

hard about something, you aren't just going to have to wrestle with ideas and evidence. You are going to need to wrestle with yourself. The uncomfortable reality is that thinking well requires effort. The real question is whether we are prepared to put in the work.

Statistics

A third and final source of insight is the modern world's love of statistics. We live in an age flooded by data. To a degree unknown by generations past, we think with statistics. Look, this weight-loss program is supported by a pie chart. This weather graph proves that climate change is false. This political issue only receives 30 per cent support in the polls.

A general rule of thumb in the art of persuasion: if in doubt, use a graph. The kids love them. Who am I kidding? We all love them. To use the language of Stephen Colbert, graphs inspire feelings of 'truthiness'. It just feels wrong to talk back to a graph. To quote the behavioural economist Aner Tal: 'the presence of even trivial graphs significantly enhances the persuasiveness of the presented claims.'

Doing statistics well actually takes quite a bit of

skill, and results must be carefully interpreted. The simple fact is you can lie with statistics without ever having to falsify the results. Allow me to give three examples.

First, perhaps the biggest problem of all: we mistake correlation for causation. There is nothing more fun than using statistics to blame or praise someone or something. Here's how. You chart two variables and show that when one goes up or down, the other does too. It is visual truthiness.

- Since we elected that political party, unemployment started rising.

- Autism rates increased as vaccine rates increased.

- People who drive Volvos have 30 per cent less crashes (they also have 50 per cent fewer friends, but that's not important right now).

This phenomenon is called correlation. But correlation is not causation. The fact that two statistics track with one another never *necessitates* that one causes the other. Indeed, if you search hard enough, you can make the most unrelated statistics correlate.

- Between 2000 and 2009 the divorce rate in the US state of Maine strongly correlated with the consumption of margarine.

- In the same 10-year period, the numbers of people who drowned by falling into a pool correlated with the number of films in which Nicolas Cage appeared. I mean, I already hated *National Treasure*, but this seals the deal.

I could go on. The point is simple. Resist the temptation to hastily use statistics to prove that this causes that.

Second, we assume all statistics are high quality. Actually, that's not entirely true. We assume statistics that *support our point of view* are all high quality.

For those of us who have never done any of this research, we have no idea how hard you must work to create meaningful numbers. In everyday rhetoric, there are few better moves than saying, 'There's this study that's been published and it says …' It really doesn't matter what comes afterwards. If there is a 'study', you've got to believe it.

Rare is the friend who asks, 'What peer-reviewed journal was this in? Do we know their polling methodology? How large was the sample?'

Nobody wants a friend like that. They are the kind of people who would go to a kindergarten to fact-check a five-year-old's PowerPoint presentation.

But … actually, you do want a friend like that,

because that friend doesn't want you to bet the farm on a dodgy bunch of numbers that might well mean nothing. A poll on Kim Kardashian's Twitter is not as reliable as one produced by Gallup. OK, you probably already knew that. But voluntary polls, like the ones run on newspaper websites, or the entire voting structure of *The Voice* – these are not reliable indices.

Third, statistics are like friends. It's good to have more than one. The clinical psychologist Seth Kalichman has coined the term 'single-study fallacy' to describe the way we often make serious and important decisions on the basis of one published report. The damage that can be wrought by the single-study fallacy is profound. It was a single study that corrupted the public health response to AIDS in Africa. It was a single study that led anxious parents to reject vaccinating their kids for fear of autism. Next time I blithely say, 'There's been a study published, and it says …', perhaps I want to heed the advice of Kalichman:

> No one scientific study ever 'proves' anything. Scientists are cautious in drawing conclusions from even a series of experiments. Science requires that independent studies replicate a finding before it is taken as fact. Even then, there is hesitation to accept replicated research findings as 'proof.'

A better way to fail

Philosophy, psychology, and statistics each offer profound insight into the myriad ways we can think poorly. This isn't a matter of us and them. We all do stupid. We make assertions without offering justifications. We let our gut ride roughshod over our thinking. We get sucked in by a graph and stop asking questions.

An underlying feature of all the insights offered above is that good thinking requires patience and effort. As Alan Jacobs says in his wonderful book *How to Think*:

> For me, the fundamental problem we have may best be described as an orientation of the will: we suffer from a settled determination to avoid thinking. Relatively few people want to think.

You can learn as many techniques or strategies as you like. But if you are not prepared to let thinking slow you down, wear you out, and make you uncomfortable, then you'll end up cutting corners. The rest of this little volume assumes you want to put some effort in.

2. NO, YOU'RE NOT ENTITLED TO YOUR OPINION

These people are witnesses to an eternal truth: you don't need to know what you're talking about in order to have an opinion.

Alex Ryrie

I spent 10 glorious years as a college lecturer in Australia. My unique task was to teach theology and ethics to musicians, graphic designers, dramatists, and ... dancers. It. Was. The. Best.

Let me be upfront about how hard I found this task. Given most of you don't know me in the flesh, I need to make clear how much I differ from dancers. Dancers are, in my humble opinion, the most sublime of athletes, capable of beauty that pierces the heart and challenges the mind. I, on the other hand, find physical coordination one of life's true challenges. My dancing resembles an octopus falling out of a tree.

When I was asked to teach dancers, I first adopted the posture of listening. It took me years of watching, reading, and listening before I understood even a fraction of their perspective. In simple terms, I needed to hear their voice.

In my classrooms, and in my life in general, I aspire to the ideal that every voice should be heard. So what I say next might sound hypocritical.

You aren't entitled to your opinion.

Give me a moment to clarify. If all you mean by 'entitled' is you are free to believe whatever you want, we are in furious agreement. Freedom of belief is a treasure.

But 'I'm entitled to my opinion' is more often a tactic for shutting down hard questions. It's equivalent to saying: 'I can say whatever I want, and you should let me get away with it.' At this point, I agree with the philosopher Patrick Stokes: 'You are not entitled to your opinion. You are only entitled to what you can argue for.'

There is a world of difference between letting someone's voice be heard and allowing someone's perspective to pass without criticism. As Stokes points out, an opinion is a belief which makes a 'serious claim to the truth'. And serious claims to the truth need to be argued for and argued about.

Just the facts?

Upon this gifted age, in its dark hour
Rains from the sky a meteoric shower
Of facts ... they lie unquestioned, uncombined.
Wisdom enough to leech us of our ill
Is daily spun; but there exists no loom
To weave it into fabric.

> *Edna St Vincent Millay,*
> *'Upon This Age, That Never Speaks Its Mind'*

Everybody loves facts. As the Australian journalist Lenore Taylor puts it: 'Facts are, for journalists, the essential ingredient, like flour for bakers or clay for sculptors.' But facts are not just for journalists. They're for everybody. This event happened. These are the crime statistics. This is what we found under the microscope.

Facts are awesome. I think everybody should have some. Because when we don't agree on the facts, or when Kellyanne Conway, Senior Counsellor to Donald Trump, talks about 'alternative facts', then you know it's going to be a long lunch.

Nevertheless, thinking does not reduce to 'just the facts'. The facts we have do not automatically generate a conclusion. Two people can see a similar set of facts and arrive at differing end points. Consider, if you will, two leading scientists.

First, we have David Attenborough, perhaps the foremost science journalist of our time. Attenborough has looked at the facts of the natural world as long and hard as anyone. The way he sees it, nature is both beautiful and brutal. And for him, the facts of science mean there likely is no God.

Second, we have Fritz Schaefer, a leading chemist at MIT who has authored over 1200 peer-reviewed papers. Schaefer also sees the facts of the natural world, in all their beauty and mystery. But he draws the opposite conclusion. He sees the natural world as evidence of a Creator.

In the main, these men would agree about many facts (admittedly, they work in different fields). So why the different conclusions? Because thinking arranges the facts, putting them together into wonderful things we call arguments.

By 'arguments' I'm not referring to what my children do when deciding who gets the window seat in the car. Not a whole lot of rationality on display there. No, an argument is when you thoughtfully combine a set of facts (what philosophers call premises) to then draw a conclusion. The idea is that if we can agree about the premises, then my *argument* shows you why my conclusion follows, or at least why my conclusion is more likely.

Good thinking needs good arguments. People should be persuaded by good arguments, as opposed to bad. As the poem by Edna St Vincent Millay suggests, we live in a world awash with facts. What we need is skill to weave those facts into a fabric. And argument is a skill. To use a trivial example – say you are talking in a hardware store with a sales assistant, and you ask them which is the best brick to use on your retaining wall. They reply: 'The most popular brick is this one.' This is not very helpful. Popularity does not guarantee truth. The majority can be wrong.

If you consult books on logic and reasoning, you will find pages and pages devoted to what are called logical fallacies. But learning such fallacies should not be an academic exercise. If we took the time to acquaint ourselves, we might learn the many ways that everyone, from advertisers all the way through to our friends, can try and convince us with dodgy persuasion.

You know what I think

I enjoy writing in cafes. There is something about the taste of coffee, the buzz of fellow diners, and the joy of not-being-in-an-office.

Cafes are filled with conversations. Lovers sharing a meal. Friends reunited after long times apart. Work colleagues needing personal interaction. The cafe isn't the library.

Spend long enough in cafes and you cannot help but overhear people sharing opinions. Emerging out of the background noise, you often hear these words: 'You know what I reckon?'

Whenever I hear that phrase, I want to adopt the brace position. It's usually the precursor to saying something outlandish, often conspiratorial, but with little argument or evidence. Happy days.

When people talk like this, they're unlikely to open the floor for Q and A. This is a mic-drop moment. The only response is a nod, or maybe even spontaneous applause. A whoop-whoop wouldn't go astray.

So imagine how much of a buzz-kill I must be to reply: 'Umm … could you just back the truck up a little and explain how you got there?'

I know what you're thinking. Going out for a coffee shouldn't require an essay.

Point taken. And point dismissed.

See, if all we were discussing was the reason my football team failed, I would chill out more. If chats over dinner were only about our favourite Christopher Nolan film, then sure, you are entitled to your opinion.

But many of our casual conversations, in person or online, concern the most serious things. This is where we talk about racism. It is where we rehearse our views on the inclusion of the disabled, the morality of adultery, the effectiveness of vaccinations, the meaning of religious freedom, and whether we might storm the Capitol building in an insurrection.

You know, trivial stuff.

Perhaps someone might say there is no harm in what I say because I have no platform. If I were behind a lectern giving official advice, or on TV speaking to a broadcast audience, then that is a problem. But I'm just spitballing with this group of friends or having Friday drinks with colleagues. I have no power. I have no influence. Indeed, in one study by Gordon Pennycook, it appears we are happy to share a story on social media even if we might not believe it ourselves.

The general theme: I'm not responsible.

But we do not realise the power we possess. In their book *Connected: The Surprising Power of Our Social Networks and How They Shape Our Lives*, sociologists Nicholas Christakis and James Fowler explore how our social interconnectedness means individual influence can translate into systemic effects. Early in the book they state:

we realized that social influence does not end with the people we know. If we affect our friends, and they affect their friends, then our own actions can potentially spread to people we have never met.

To adopt the language of Christakis and Fowler, connection enables contagion (in both good and bad ways). We cannot know the ways our thinking may go viral. And the effects of our influence go beyond the content of our thinking; they even extend to its manner. There is research to suggest the posture of arrogance can become contagious. Joey Cheng, a psychologist at York University, posits that if you have been exposed to an overconfident thinker, you are then more likely to overestimate your own cognitive abilities.

These problems have been magnified in the digital age. As the journalist Cullen Murphy puts it, 'When people can publish whatever they want, they do.' Movements have been formed from tweets. People have been sacked because of Facebook. It is a world of wondrous, and terrifying, potential.

In August 2020, *The Guardian* reported that the Scots language version of Wikipedia had been compromised by the amateur contributions of a schoolkid. Scots is one of the literary languages of the British Isles. Rarely used now, it is important in the study of writers past, including the poet

Robert Burns. For seven years a teenager from North Carolina was assiduously editing the Scots entries, eventually affecting a staggering 49 per cent of contributions. There was only one problem – the young man did not really understand the language. The disastrous result was branded by some an act of 'cultural vandalism'.

When people can publish whatever they want, they do.

Given such power and potentiality, should you maybe think a little before dropping that intemperate rant? Should you give it five minutes, or perhaps five days, before you send out that conspiratorial tweet? Should you edit that Wikipedia entry just a little more carefully?

You are responsible for your thinking. That doesn't mean you can control everything of how your ideas might be communicated, translated, and construed. But it does mean you have an effect. And thinking well means acting wisely with the bits we can control.

Ideas are power

What exactly are we doing when we share our thinking with someone else?

Thinking often starts as self-expression. If I

want to know you then I want to know what you think. We sometimes share our thoughts with no other goal than saying, 'This is me.'

But at least some of the time, and perhaps a lot more than you realise, you are sharing your ideas because you want others to agree with you. And for them to change as a result. Your opinion on good parenting is more than a personal mission statement; you wish others would do it better. When you share a link on Facebook, attend a community meeting on a proposed property development, speak up at the work meeting – you want to change minds and affect lives.

If we define power very basically as the ability to form or transform, then ideas are power. Even yours. To influence someone's thinking, to change someone's mind, to reorient someone's worldview, makes a tangible difference. Therefore, the way I wield my intellect should be in the same way I wield my physical strength. Carefully. Respectfully. With full awareness of the benefits I can provide, and the damage I can do.

If you don't know what you're talking about, admit it. You can still say your piece, but perhaps ask it as a question, or use the language of 'I'm wondering if …' Take responsibility for how you throw your intellectual weight around. Thinking well is everyone's concern because somebody's listening. Someone might change their mind. And then there are two of you. And then four of you. And so on.

Changing even one person's thinking is significant, no matter how small it may seem. It reminds me of the story of the old man who comes across a young boy on a beach, surrounded by hundreds of starfish which have been washed ashore. One by one, the young boy is throwing the starfish back into the sea. The old man protests that the boy's efforts are futile, that there must be hundreds if not thousands of starfish, and that his efforts make no difference.

The boy's response? He bends down to pick up another starfish, tosses it into the sea, and says simply: 'It made a difference to that one.'

The problem of disrespect

'You are not entitled to your opinion' means when you share your ideas it's still OK for people to ask questions, offer critique, and suggest improvements. This is the very definition of critical thinking.

The word 'critical' has a negative valence in our culture. To be critical equates to tearing down, demeaning, and attacking. That's not how I, and many others, conceive of the term. In the words of Richard Paul, 'Critical thinking is the art of analyzing and evaluating thinking with a view to improving it.' Criticism is less about destroying your ideas and more about what the philosopher Catherine Hundleby calls 'argument repair'. When we pull apart each other's thinking, we should be trying to help. That's what love aims at.

There is no denying that having your opinion questioned is uncomfortable. Our practice of thinking is one of the ways we try to belong. In the same way we might alter our appearance in order to fit in, our thinking is just as susceptible. Our convictions, and even the language we adopt, become markers for inclusion within a tribe. So to have our ideas questioned feels disrespectful. It is tantamount to saying, 'You don't belong.'

But what if the highest respect I can pay to you is to question your ideas with a view to improving them? What if our friendship did not rely on you (or me) being right all the time, but on both of us helping each other to think?

Perhaps the people we want as friends are those who ask better questions rather than those who agree on all the answers.

A better way to share opinions

At the start of this little book, I asked the question: 'Do we think only for ourselves, or do we think for the good of others?' In a few chapters I am going to lay out my own take on how to think humbly, think hospitably, and think with love in your heart. But at this juncture let me point out that as soon as you acknowledge ideas are powerful, then the question of love cannot be far away. Love becomes clear in the way we wield power and the way we seek to empower others. That's true in both body and mind.

We have a duty *to each other* to think as well as we can. Because you matter, I want to think better. *For you.*

As a pastor and an educator, I can't count the number of times somebody has told me that an idea I shared, a sentence I wrote, or a talk I gave made a positive difference in their life. And in so many cases the influential moment has not been from a platform, where I was giving prepared remarks. It was a random conversation, a short question after class, or an article I recommended via email. And it changed someone's world. What made the difference was being in the habit of being thoughtful.

By the same token, I am also aware of people

who have been damaged by another person's ideas, including my own. A Facebook post that sent someone down a conspiracy rabbit-hole. A dinner party where hasty answers were given to complex questions. People spouting off the first thing that came into their mind or trading off their reputation even in the absence of proper qualifications. And it changed someone's life. For the worse.

Our voice matters, but when I raise my voice, it means taking responsibility. A mind can be an instrument for love or a weapon for wounding.

Choose love.

3. PUTTING EXPERTS IN THEIR PLACE

The talent quest is a perennial favourite of broadcast television. With long-running dramas migrating to Netflix and Disney+, the broadcast schedule is now filled with the rags-to-riches opportunities of 'audition entertainment'. Fancy yourself a cook? Then try *MasterChef* or *The Great British Bake Off*. Believe in your heart you're an interior designer? Then join the brawl at *Grand Designs* or *House Rules*.

But the gold standard remains the singing contest.

Pretty much everyone sings. Only some of us can sing well.

This basic dichotomy underpins a thousand hours of television. The genre of 'tournament singing' exists to capture two basic phenomena – the inspirational diamond-in-the-rough and the catastrophic failure.

The inspirational diamond is the fan favourite. Here is the overlooked guy or girl whose voice has been hitherto hidden, now bursting upon the stage. Even better if they are a truck driver who sings opera, or a granny who does hip-hop. The larger the incongruity, the more our hearts are melted.

But the catastrophic failure is equally essential. There are not enough 'once-in-a-generation' singers to fill out the billable hours. For the sake of entertainment, we need – nay, we want – to see the tone-deaf, the sonically challenged, and the clueless suburban girl who thinks she is the next Pink when really she is Paris Hilton.

The catastrophic failure works best when they lack all self-awareness. In the backstage preamble that precedes their performance, they tell the camera this is their moment. A prodigious talent will be unveiled. They enter stage right, the music swells, they open their mouth – at which point reality intrudes.

Humans chronically overestimate their abilities. Ethan Zell, a professor of psychology, puts it bluntly: 'If you give people a questionnaire where they rate themselves relative to the average, almost everyone in the class thinks they're above average at almost everything.'

This is the cognitive bias of illusory superiority.

It's why most of us think we are a good driver.

It's why too many of us think we can pull off a podcast.

It's why your friend's side hustle was a business disaster.

And it's why so many of us, from novice through to seasoned veteran, end up thinking poorly. In this chapter, I want to suggest that human beings easily fall into two traps:

- Everybody thinks they're an expert.
- We place too much faith in experts.

On the surface, this might appear a contradiction. By the end, I hope to have shown that these two can go together. Or perhaps humans don't make sense. There's always that.

Everybody's an expert

In 2013, a young woman took to Twitter to ask for help on a chemistry assignment. She needed to find answers on the deadly nerve agent sarin. Dan Kaszeta, an internationally recognised expert on chemical weapons, jumped on to give her some helpful tips. But this included him *correcting* some of her basic factual errors. Her response? She swore at him, derided him as ignorant, and told him to shut up (you realise I'm sanitising this, don't you?).

In 1999 Justin Kruger and David Dunning conducted a series of experiments assessing self-awareness of competence. Can people accurately predict their skill levels?

The answer? Not so much. To use the study's own words, many of us 'reach erroneous conclusions and make unfortunate choices, but [our] incompetence robs [us] of the ability to realize it'.

And so was born the 'Dunning-Kruger' effect.

The Dunning-Kruger effect shows that thinking well requires healthy awareness of our inadequacies. And in no place is this more obvious than when we talk about expertise.

What does it mean to be 'knowledgeable' about something?

Growing up in a world where education is a democratic imperative, you hopefully were taught the value of thinking for yourself. This is a vital skill. So long as you understand that thinking for yourself is *not* equivalent to attaining knowledge. On the contrary, learning to think for yourself should inculcate reverence for how hard it is to be 'knowledgeable' about anything. As Tom Nichols points out, 'Higher education is supposed to cure us of the false belief that everyone is as smart as everyone else. Unfortunately … rather than disabusing students of their intellectual solipsism, the modern university ends up reinforcing it.'

In distinction from the past, we live in an information-rich environment. Hence the frequent calls for people to 'do your own research'. The digital world offers us a near endless supply of information we can use and abuse to support what we already believe. But information alone does not, in and of itself, constitute research.

The key to researching something well is not simply finding information; it's finding *quality* information. And here there is one important principle to remember.

The internet is not a library.

It is a dumping ground.

A good library is a place where professionally trained curators have carefully considered what is best. Whereas the internet is like hard-rubbish days on your local street. Everybody brings out their stuff, most of which is useless junk, but sometimes you find a lava lamp to die for.

When I was a child, my dad worked for a printer who published legal texts. During my summer holidays, I tagged along to work with him, sitting in rooms filled with law textbooks. For some bizarre reason, I'm still not allowed to practise law. Apparently, the mere presence of information does not confer the ability to use it well.

In 2015 a team of psychologists from Yale University conducted studies demonstrating that people routinely mistake 'access to information for their own personal understanding of the information'. As Tom Nichols quips, there is an 'illusion of expertise provided by a limitless supply of facts'.

First impressions aren't always the best. When I wrote my PhD, I thought I already knew my topic well. But after a year of researching, I was more confused than when I began. I was learning how little I knew. It wasn't until well into my second year of study that some clarity began to emerge.

When I tell this story to many different friends, some of them see it as a parable of all that is wrong about education. Academics just make simple things hard. How could you read for a year and be more confused?

Because life is complex, thinking is a skill, and the best kind of expertise requires patience and humility. Or as the African-American biblical scholar Esau McCaulley puts it: 'It's okay not to have a strong opinion about a nuanced policy issue that you learned about 48 hours ago. It's fine to read and think and reflect.'

Putting too much faith in experts

In 1949, the Portuguese neurologist Antonio Egas Moniz shared the Nobel Prize for Medicine. His achievement? Moniz invented the lobotomy, the surgical procedure in which mentally ill patients are treated by slicing into the prefrontal cortex of the brain. In the middle part of the 20th century lobotomies were a popular method for treating those suffering from depression, schizophrenia, and OCD.

Perhaps the most infamous practitioner was an American psychiatrist by the name of Walter Freeman. His method of transorbital lobotomy involved driving an ice-pick through a patient's eye socket, at which point Dr Freeman would wiggle the pick back and forth, *inside their brain*.

The procedure took all of 10 minutes.

But it ruined some people forever.

A common outcome was the patient being reduced to a 'surgically induced childhood' (Freeman's phrase). In one horrifying postoperative report, Freeman wrote about a 29-year-old woman as a 'smiling, lazy, and satisfactory patient with the personality of an oyster'.

What is the point of such a gruesome anecdote? Sometimes, experts get it wrong. Like, really wrong.

Despite our illusions of competence all of us have to rely on another's expertise for many aspects of our life. I don't know how to build a house, perform a colonoscopy, or bake French pastries. There is no generically 'smart' person whose answers are equally insightful no matter the topic. To quote Steven Levitt and Stephen Dubner:

just because you're great at something doesn't mean you're good at everything. Unfortunately, this fact is routinely ignored by those who engage in – take a deep breath – ultracrepidarianism, or 'the habit of giving opinions and advice on matters outside of one's knowledge or competence.'

Ultracrepidarianism. Now there's a word to try at home.

Truth be told, we all know very little about a lot. We necessarily rely on the wisdom of others.

Faced with this situation, we sometimes play a game called 'pick your favoured expert'. This has been evident throughout the COVID pandemic. The arrival of a new virus in pretty much every country in the world meant platforming a whole new set of experts. Epidemiologists became Instagram influencers. Daily newspapers reported that 'a leading doctor has recommended …' or 'a senior economist has predicted …' It was Sweden versus New Zealand. Herd immunity versus elimination. My Twitter feed blew up with links to articles proving we should be doing this, followed one tweet later with another expert suggesting the *exact opposite*.

Drowning in an ocean of contested commentary, expertise gets weaponised. We subcontract our preferred 'authority' for the purposes of confirmation bias. We selectively quote experts as a way to verify our prejudices, defend our gut response, and avoid thinking carefully. As Nate Silver puts it:

the more information you have, the more selective you can be in which information you pick out to tell the narrative that might not be true or accurate, or the one that helps your business, but the one that makes you feel good or that your friends agree with.

This behaviour towards experts easily ignores two important truths. First, *all* experts get some things wrong. Even Tom Nichols' book *The Death of Expertise*, which is primarily about how we too easily dismiss expert knowledge, is candid enough to include a chapter detailing when experts go wrong. Nutritionists changed their opinion on eating eggs. Political analysts failed to anticipate the dismantling of the USSR.

Nowhere is expert failure more apparent than in the messy world of prediction. For more than 30 years the political scientist Philip Tetlock has assessed the quality and accuracy of expert predictions. The results? 'The average expert [is] roughly as accurate as a dart-throwing chimpanzee.'

The second truth we ignore is that experts disagree. If you work within any academic field, part of the price of admission is that you must acknowledge and fairly respond to very smart people who disagree with you. This is why academics use footnotes and expect questions at conferences. It is how peer review is meant to work. With the exception of the chemical structure of water or the intelligence of Einstein, most ideas are debated. What Tom Nichols says about science could be said about thinking in general: thinking is a 'process, not a conclusion'. Therefore, the mere fact that you can find one professor who challenges the consensus is hardly earth-shattering, but neither is it unimportant. We learn best when we realise that no one person has all the answers.

A better expertise: The value of intellectual humility

Human beings tend to either overrate their competence or rely too heavily on (selected) experts. The common denominator between these behaviours is the absence of humility. Sometimes the hardest thing to do can be to acknowledge our limitations. As Steven Levitt and Stephen Dubner say, the three hardest words in the English language are 'I Don't Know.' If you ask me to comment on classical ballet, my first obligation is to admit my ignorance. Even on subjects where I'm marginally better, such as US politics, I *should* remind you that my ideas are amateur at best.

Humility remains a problem even when you graduate from novice. The worst kind of expert is the one who offers their opinion with no acknowledgement that they *could* be wrong.

Which, by the way, is precisely the kind of expert favoured by the media.

Television and Twitter don't want nuance. They want provocation. And the reason for this is disturbingly simple. There are strong incentives to make bold and alarming statements, and relatively few incentives to keep track of whether those statements prove to be true. To cite Levitt and Dubner again: 'the cost of saying "I don't know" is higher than the cost of being wrong.'

In my college classrooms, I tried to develop the habit of telling my class that at least some of what I was teaching them was incorrect. The problem was I didn't know which bits, otherwise I would fix them. But I wanted to remind my students that my thinking could always be improved, including by them.

Perhaps I might seem pessimistic about knowing and learning. In fact, the opposite is true. Over time, I have learnt a great deal. I know way more at 44 than at 14. But the key to learning was the humility to first admit ignorance. As Socrates once put it: 'I seem, then, in just this little thing to be wiser than this man at any rate, that what

I do not know I do not think I know either.' The 18th-century poet Alexander Pope said something perhaps even more important: 'A man should never be ashamed to own he has been in the wrong, which is but saying ... that he is wiser today than he was yesterday.'

Despite all his research demonstrating the predictive failure of experts, Philip Tetlock has remained optimistic for better outcomes. He believes that experts can make wise and helpful predictions. Among his many suggestions for improving forecasting, it is interesting to see how humility features. Tetlock talks of the need to own our mistakes, to admit our levels of doubt, to identify counterarguments, and to update our beliefs as evidence accumulates.

Simply put, intellectual humility requires that we follow the advice of Alan Jacobs to 'value learning over debating'. The expert you can trust is not the one who shouts the loudest. The expert you can trust is the one who lays out what they know while also laying out what they don't know. Those are the kind of people who likely have your best in mind. Because when it comes to expertise, you aren't just looking for the right ideas. You're also looking for good people you can trust. Because they're the ones who will tell you when they got it wrong.

4. FINDING CONFIDENCE, NOT CERTAINTY

In the modern world the stupid are cocksure while the intelligent are full of doubt.

Bertrand Russell

I remember asking my wife to marry me. We had known each other for many years and discussed the possibility for many months. I felt certain that marriage was a great idea. Yet once I popped the question a gnawing hole developed in my stomach. I'd jumped off a cliff into a world of unknowns.

If I was so sure about my decision, why was I feeling funny?

Such feelings are a persistent presence in our life. We feel it when we buy a house. Accept a job. Send our kids to school. Vote for that candidate. Go in for surgery. No matter how sure we are, we cannot eliminate doubt.

The human desire for certainty lies behind one of the foundational moments in modern philosophy. In the 17th century the philosopher René Descartes resolved to question everything he knew, in an attempt to find a bedrock truth immune from doubt.

- Can we be certain about what we see and hear? No, said Descartes – we've all been tricked by our senses at one time or another.

- Can we be certain that we are awake? Not really, given that sometimes we've mistaken a dream for real life.

Proceeding methodically, Descartes ended up eviscerating nearly every claim to certainty.

So is there anything we can be sure of? Well … even as I am doubting everything, I cannot doubt that I exist. If I am doubting, then I am thinking, and so I must exist as 'some kind of thinking thing'. This is the back-story behind the immortal phrase 'I think, therefore I am (*cogito ergo sum*)'. For Descartes this seemed like a breakthrough. I'm still dubious.

I still feel some butterflies about most of my decisions. I'm not totally sure how to respond to a global pandemic. When the anaesthetist pops a needle in my arm, it still feels like some sort of risk. *Contra* Descartes, I just can't nail certainty. Questions always remain.

The way to confidence

Despite my best efforts, there seems little that is *impossible* to doubt.

- Do you know *for certain* that your car brakes won't fail?

- Do you know *for certain* that your partner loves you?

- Do you know *for certain* that your eyes are not deceiving you?

If unquestionable certainty is my standard for knowing, and deciding, then I am unlikely to make it to work each morning, let alone find someone to marry me.

Pushed to its extremes, we could end up with a false dichotomy – either we can know things for certain, or we can't know anything at all. We become dogmatists or sceptics. But neither outlook is helpful.

Proving any belief to the point where it is impossible to doubt would take an amount of time and effort that is practically impossible, and still it probably could not be done.

Earlier in this book I talked about the unhelpful ways we try to use (and abuse) statistics as a way of proving our point. We love statistics because they give us a feeling of certainty – the solidity of 'hard' data. But we would do well to heed the warning of the economist Sarah Hamersma:

> Everyone wants the numbers to tell them what is going on, what makes sense, what to do next. Intelligent, capable people feign an inability to understand nuance that is actually just an unwillingness to tolerate it. While the data need statistical analysis to make them informative, even that analysis still requires an interpreter – and everyone would like that interpreter to be certain. The use of numbers instead of words can give the illusion that she is.

But this doesn't mean we can't know anything or make good decisions.

What we are looking for is confidence, not certainty. Human beings have the capacity to know *enough*. Enough to be confident in our beliefs. In actual fact, this is what most people mean when they say they are certain about something. As the theologian John Stackhouse defines it:

> I think it's fine to say that I am 'certain' about these things. When I do, I am reporting on my state of mind. I am saying that I am so highly convinced of them that I entertain no serious doubts about them. I think, and feel, and act with untroubled confidence in them.

In our confidence, it remains possible we are wrong. Nevertheless, if we have legitimate confidence, we can act upon what we know.

The advantages of confidence (and the problems of certainty)

Preferring the language of confidence over certainty is beneficial in many different ways. Let me suggest just a few.

First, pursuing legitimate confidence in our beliefs encourages us to find good reasons. Here we might cite the example of religious belief, which people frequently misconstrue as an irrational leap in the dark. To quote John Stackhouse again:

> No one exercises 'blind faith' in anything or anyone. Everyone has a reason to believe what he or she believes, even if someone else thinks it to be an insufficient reason, and even if that belief turns out to be a mistake.

What is true for religious knowledge is true more generally of all knowledge. The impossibility of final certainty does not invalidate the task of finding grounds for our convictions.

Second, you can be confident in your ideas without having to shut down questions. If we operate from the principle of absolute certainty, then when people express scepticism, it triggers us. The assumption is: if my idea can be questioned, it must not be right. But, in truth, even the best and surest ideas can be questioned. It does not mean they are not right. Reframed in this way, good questions become an opportunity for demonstrating your confidence, with gentleness and respect. And maybe, just maybe, your thinking might be improved. Contrary to what we might first assume, *a truly confident thinker welcomes good questions.*

Third, once we understand that we should expect confidence, not certainty, we can see why some people will never be convinced. A standard gambit in so many arguments is for someone to demand a level of proof which isn't possible.

'I'll believe in human-induced climate change when you prove it beyond question.'

'I won't believe in God unless I can be absolutely certain.'

'I won't have that vaccine unless you can eliminate all doubt that it is safe.'

All of the above discussions require important decisions where we must eventually act. And in each case, I cannot eliminate *every* doubt. I have to make my call with my limited brain.

There is *always* wriggle room in a debate. Despite the confident presentation you might give, citing all the best evidence, your conversation partner can always reply that it is all just fake news, or there is a single study that disproves all the others, or there is this one thing your theory cannot explain.

We make decisions with imperfect information. That requires us to do two things:

- Eventually make a call, by picking the idea we think is the best.

- Allow for the possibility that we could be wrong.

Generally speaking, we cannot find evidence which makes our beliefs necessary. Rather, we are looking for sufficient evidence to be confident in our beliefs. We need *enough* reasons.

The problem is, there is no official board of 'enoughness' to tell us when we have appropriate reason to warrant a decision, a belief, or whatever else. What is 'enough' for me may differ from what is 'enough' for you. At the very least, we should be able to offer good reasons for our confidence. But we also need to be awake to the way our confidence might result from cowardice.

A better confidence: Intellectual courage

In his 1997 book *The Last Word*, the atheist philosopher Thomas Nagel offers this deeply honest reflection:

> I want atheism to be true … It isn't just that I don't believe in God and, naturally, hope that I'm

right in my belief. It's that I hope there is no God! I don't want there to be a God; I don't want the universe to be like that.

I do not present Nagel's point here as something peculiar to atheism. We're all like Nagel at least some of the time, where truth becomes a function of our desires, not just our thoughts.

There does come a point in some conversations when you can rightly say back to someone: 'I get the feeling that whatever reasons I offer you, it will never be enough. Perhaps you just don't *want* to believe this idea.'

I do not recommend pulling this trigger early. It is not a weapon to be brandished carelessly. But sometimes we have to name the elephant – that there are some things we just do not want to be true. Whatever you think about climate change, Al Gore was onto something when he called his environmental documentary *An Inconvenient Truth*. Many truths are uncomfortable, because if we believed them, then everything would change.

Part of the challenge of thinking is that it is never just theoretical. As the American writer Steven Garber puts it:

We are not, first of all, philosophers, consciously theorizing about the universe – even philosophers are not that. Human beings that we are, we are choosers, choosing how we will live. It is our longings and loves that form us, most deeply, forming what we believe about what is real and true and right – with complexity and mystery. And so there are no cheap answers to the questions of life because there are no cheap questions about life, and if we imagine otherwise, we are badly mistaken.

To use another insight from Garber, our thinking implicates us. If something is true, then life will be different. And what happens if that difference confuses, upsets, or challenges me?

Thinking requires courage. This is the case all the way through the thinking process. At the beginning, the preparedness to admit ignorance requires bravery. Socially, it would be easier to always nod and smile, and act like I know what I'm talking about. We can then avoid asking the dumb question – you know, the one where you admit you haven't a clue what everyone is talking about, and everyone stares like you've just confessed your love of the piano accordion.

But as you grow in your thinking, and in your confidence, a different dimension of courage has to emerge. This is the courage of responding to what you learn. If thinking gone wrong manifests in confirmation bias, then thinking done right should do the opposite – it should unsettle us. Finding truth means moments of surprise, the regular experience where your gut instincts are disconfirmed.

If the words *I thought this was the case, but the truth is much different* have never passed your lips, you're probably not thinking really well. Little wonder that Alan Jacobs concludes his 'Thinking Person's Checklist' with just two words:

Be brave.

5. THE CHARACTER OF A THINKER: HUMILITY, HOSPITALITY, LOVE

Perhaps you regard this thinking about myself as a waste of time – but how can I be a logician before I'm a human being! Far the most important thing is to settle accounts with myself!

Ludwig Wittgenstein

In their book *Metaphors We Live By*, George Lakoff and Mark Johnson point to the way we configure argument in terms of warfare. We debate *opponents*. We *attack* their points. That argument was *on target*. When you drop a stinging line on Twitter, the preferred hashtag is #ShotsFired.

This tells us plenty about our ideal thinker. They have *mastered* their topic, they *dominate* the discourse, they're *crushing* it. Is it any wonder that being a thinker is associated with pride, arrogance, and feelings of elite superiority? Thinking is power, and you use power for victory.

In my high school years I was educated at a school for the academically gifted. Truth be told, it was a wonderful environment, and I'm mostly better for the experience. But among the many lessons I imbibed was how to be an intellectual athlete. My life became consumed by academic rankings, in which every exam was an Olympic event, and everybody else a competitor. No matter my attempts to expunge it, that adversarial disposition remains two decades later. I still instinctually scan the room to ask: who do I have to beat?

Lurking beneath the chapters in this book has been a drumbeat. I have tried to suggest that thinking does not merely expose our intelligence. It unveils our character. Intelligence isn't simply a matter of what to think. It's also *how* you think and *why* you think.

The virtue of thinking

The idea of virtue might seem old-fashioned, more at home in a Jane Austen novel. But it's actually a popular idea in modern ethical discussion. 'Virtue ethics' tries to move us from thinking of ethics as just making right or wrong *decisions* to instead focus on a person's *character*. The best kind of ethics is where someone does the right thing because they're the right kind of person.

At first it seems strange to apply the language of virtue to thinking. Isn't character revealed in moral practices like resisting corruption and giving to the poor? Yes, indeed. But the way we practise thinking is just as much an indicator of who we really are. As the philosopher Jason Baehr puts it:

> a fully or broadly virtuous person can … be counted on to care deeply about ends like truth, knowledge, evidence, rationality, and understanding; and out of this fundamental concern will emerge other traits like inquisitiveness, carefulness and thoroughness in inquiry, fair-mindedness, open-mindedness, and intellectual patience, honesty, courage, humility, and rigor.

A virtuous mind *cares* about thinking. In an earlier chapter I suggested that good thinking requires hard work. There is effort required to counteract our biases. If you are going to think well, you have to *want* to think. You *desire* the truth. If these dispositions are absent, then the temptation will be to just *use* thinking. It becomes an instrument of power, a lever for social advancement, a garment you wear in order to belong.

Let's be honest. Being thoughtful can get annoying. It often stands in the way of the easy option. It will slow some decisions down, and it may stop some altogether.

But the relevance of virtue goes even further. Thinking operates best when nested within a virtuous life. It needs patient effort, a willingness to take responsibility, and considerable bravery.

The importance of character means we need a moral vision, a template if you will, that defines what it means to be truly human. At this point we can be candid and admit we don't all agree about what that good life is. As I indicated at the start, my own moral vision is grounded in the Christian tradition and focused on the example of Jesus. Yet even if you don't identify as Christian, Jesus might well have influenced you. As the historian Tom Holland says:

> To live in a Western country is to live in a society still utterly saturated by Christian concepts and assumptions. This is no less true for Jews or Muslims than it is for Catholics or Protestants. Two thousand years on from the birth of Christ, it does not require a belief that he rose from the dead to be stamped by the formidable – indeed the inescapable – influence of Christianity … its trace elements are to be found everywhere in the West.

With due acknowledgement of my Christian assumptions, I want to offer three virtuous practices: Humility, Hospitality, and Love. And for each I want to explore how they might impact how we think.

Humility

We spoke about intellectual humility in chapter 3. Humility keeps us aware of our limitations, open to the possibility that we are wrong, and cognizant of our need for further learning.

The Christian story (along with the beliefs of Judaism and Islam) sees human beings as both finite and fallible. This provides an explanation for why humility is fundamental. Our finitude derives from the fact that we are creatures, not the Creator. Therefore, human beings cannot possess God-like knowledge because they are not God. Human knowledge is powerful, but it is also partial.

Added to this finitude is fallibility. Human beings, no matter how wonderful, are prone to go against what is good – not only what is good for themselves, but also what is good for others. Within a religious vocabulary this is called sin. Sin is not a popular word these days, but it actually neatly captures, among other things, the ways in which our behaviour frequently does harm to ourselves and others. It should not surprise us that our thinking can become co-opted for evil purposes, where we think poorly, think selfishly, and where truth becomes a tactic just to get what we want.

In theory this belief should lead to the practice of humility. If it is true that we are finite and fallible, then it is worth asking questions of our thinking – its motives, its arguments, its outcomes. I should question myself. And I should question others too. None of us gets it right all the time. We think best by thinking together.

This is perhaps the right time to say a brief something about conspiracy theories and the people who love them. Although conspiracy theories are often celebrated as the revolt of the little person against arrogant elites, this obscures a crucial fact. Conspiracy theorists are often the least humble people of all. Far from acknowledging what they do not know or admitting the possibility of error, conspiracy theorists think they can explain everything.

Hospitality

Hospitality is a word not often applied to thinking. In contemporary language, hospitality describes an industry (hotels, restaurants) or dinner parties with friends. In the modern age, hospitality is transactional. But there is a rich tradition of thinking, in both religion and philosophy, which frames hospitality in more challenging ways. In my own Christian tradition, hospitality is about loving and welcoming *the stranger*.

Traditionally, hospitality is associated with the home and the dinner table. You welcome the stranger by offering them shelter and a meal. But being hospitable can be so much more. The political theologian Luke Bretherton suggests hospitality is a posture we can adopt towards those with whom we disagree. This is something far better than tolerance. Tolerance addresses our differences by saying 'let's agree to disagree'. I will *permit* you to believe that. That is helpful, but it's far from generous. Hospitality, on the other hand, welcomes the stranger, making space for the foreigner to become a friend.

Being intellectually hospitable means seeing other minds as strangers we can offer welcome to. Hospitality opens a space for ideas to be aired and perspectives to be discussed and understood. It is important to say, hospitality does not confuse welcome with agreement. Here is the sticking point for so many. If I patiently listen, then it must mean I agree. This seems predicated on the idea that if I disagree, I must shout early and shout often.

Perhaps one of commonest laments in contemporary culture is the problem of 'echo chambers'. Living in a world of curated news feeds and on-demand television, we are the masters of our informational world. Technologies keep getting better at screening out the difficult, the different, the challenging, and the inconvenient. The result? In 2019, the think-tank More in Common found that the *more* politically engaged we are, and the *greater* our consumption of news media, the more likely we are to misunderstand the views of our opponents.

The French historian Marc Bloch put it well: 'It is so easy to denounce. We are never sufficiently understanding.' We despise one another without ever knowing what the *other* believes. But you don't need to start shouting before they've finished. Listening does not constitute affirmation, and understanding does not constitute endorsement. A virtuous thinker works from the principle that you cannot critique a position you do not understand.

So how might you show charity to those you disagree with? Here is a helpful first step: 'steelman' their arguments. Steelmanning, a term coined by the atheist blogger Chana Messinger, is 'seeking out the best form of the other person's argument, even if it's not the one they presented'.

Steelmanning is not only a hospitable action. It is a pragmatic one as well. There are few better ways of demonstrating that truth is your priority. The stronger I make your argument, the more it improves mine. After all, it could be my opponent is right. Maybe my argument needs repair. So in the end, everyone benefits. Hospitable discussion prioritises blessing the culture, rather than just winning arguments.

Love

Undergirding and surrounding all that I have said is the practice of love. In the Christian tradition, love is supreme. At the centre of God's attributes is love, a love which extends even to his enemies. Accordingly, love is at the centre of Christian virtue, for it is the compass point by which *all* actions are to be oriented and against which all actions are to be judged.

Love is not the counterpoint of thinking and truth; love is the goal. My practice of thinking and desire for truth is *in order that* I might love others well. Being right is unworthy as an end in itself. If all I care about is being right, then in the middle of an argument, faced with the terrifying prospect that I might lose, I will do literally anything to win.

This might include petty insults and shouting, but for some it will extend to violence, both threatened and real.

My goal is to love my neighbour through thinking well. Of course, I hope that I am right. But if I discover, painfully, that it is I who am in error, then all is not lost.

Humility reminds me how we can often be wrong or how a different perspective can shed better light on an idea that I hold.

Hospitality reminds me that strangers can become friends.

And love? Love constrains me to ask what is best, not only for me, but also for others.

CONCLUSION: CONFESSIONS OF AN IMPERFECT FRIEND

I have loved *knowing* for a very long time. My mum will tell you that, from primary school onwards, I was an arrogant little pain in the neck because I always wanted to be the smartest. I really, really love being right.

For all the cautions I've offered in this book, I'm fundamentally optimistic that people can think well and find truth. As my friend and colleague Natasha Moore puts it: 'may you have the pessimism to look steadily and unflinchingly at the problems, and the optimism to perceive and pursue the opportunities hiding behind them.'

When it comes to thinking, I'm much better than I used to be, but far from the finished product. I still aspire to be clever. I still enjoy being right. But slowly, I am learning to think not only for myself but also for the good of others.

Inevitably that means learning how to navigate disagreement. Even the best of friends will find themselves at loggerheads over an idea. You think differently. And only one of you can be right (although keep in mind that both of you might be wrong).

One available option is to quickly play the 'let's agree to disagree' card. Fair enough. If your chosen topic is favourite ice cream flavours or whether LeBron James is basketball's GOAT, then go right ahead. But at other times and for many topics, love for one another compels us to *persuasion*. We owe it to ourselves and each other to seek to change minds, and in turn to allow our own mind to be changed, while maintaining friendship.

And here I must confess how much I've been an imperfect friend. I've said too little. And I've said too much. Finding my Goldilocks moment where my words are 'just right' so easily proves elusive. And yet if we cannot learn to voice our disagreements and learn truth together, then we are much the poorer for being right in our own eyes.

In a 2015 presentation to college students addressing the problem of 'argument culture', the communications professor Tim Muehlhoff suggested a series of four questions to ask in any conversation.

- What does this person believe?

- Why does this person believe?

- Where do we agree?

- With this person, at this time, under these circumstances, what is the one thing I should say?

That last question always gets me. *With this person, at this time, under these circumstances, what is the one thing I should say?*

Thinking well is a habit, progressing mostly in increments, with many setbacks and failures. But progress we can if we have love enough to speak and courage enough to listen. It requires patience and persistence. As the philosopher Ludwig Wittgenstein puts it:

> The truth can be spoken only by someone who is already at home in it; not by someone who still lives in falsehood and reaches out from falsehood to truth on just one occasion.

May you find truth to be your home. I wish you well and look forward to learning from you.

Re:CONSIDERING

NOTES

INTRODUCTION

Page 3: René Descartes famously defined. You can find Descartes' musings in places like his *Meditations on First Philosophy.* My volume is René Descartes, *The Philosophical Works of Descartes,* Volume 1 (Cambridge University Press, Cambridge, 1967), pp. 144–57.

Page 4: Modern Westerners live in what Peter Drucker has dubbed a 'knowledge economy'. Drucker introduced this term in chapter 12 of his book *The Age of Discontinuity: Guidelines to Our Changing Society* (Harper & Row, New York, 1969).

Page 4: The German philosopher Immanuel Kant. This is from Kant's famous essay 'What Is Enlightenment?' I used the translation of Lewis White Beck in Immanuel Kant, *Foundations of the Metaphysics of Morals, and What Is Enlightenment?* (Liberal Arts Press, New York, 1959).

Page 4: 'Idiot brain' happens even in the little things. I'm taking some of these phrases from the large number of books which seem devoted to exposing how dumb we can be. Books like Dean Burnett, *The Idiot Brain: A Neuroscientist Explains What Your Head Is Really Up To* (Faber & Faber, London, 2016) or Carol Tavris and Elliot Aronson, *Mistakes Were Made (But Not by Me): Why We Justify Foolish Beliefs, Bad Decisions, and Hurtful Acts* (2nd edn, Pinter and Martin, London, 2013).

1. A THOUSAND WAYS TO FALL

Page 9: Philosophers press us to consider. If you're feeling courageous and would like to try your hand at some philosophy, you could have a crack at Robert Audi, *Epistemology: A Contemporary Introduction to the Theory of Knowledge* (Routledge, New York, 2010). At a much more popular level, and a personal favourite of mine, has been James W. Sire, *Why Should Anyone Believe Anything at All?* (InterVarsity, Downers Grove, 1994).

Page 10: the real movers and shakers have been psychologists. If you want a good summary of some of these ideas, grab Ben Yagoda's article 'Your Lying Mind' in the September 2018 edition of *The Atlantic*.

Page 11: The social psychologist Jonathan Haidt argues. This is one of the central theses of Haidt's *The Righteous Mind* (Allen Lane, London, 2012).

Page 11: One of the chief ways our gut influences thinking. This is nicely introduced in chapter 1 of Haidt's *The Righteous Mind*. But if you want another gem of a chapter, then take a look at chapter 3 in Alan Jacobs, *How to Think: A Guide for the Perplexed* (Profile, London, 2017).

Page 12: Daniel Kahneman talks about. Kahneman's classic book is *Thinking Fast and Slow* (Allen Lane, London, 2011). You would do well to read it patiently.

Page 12: As Erin Devers and Jason Runyan put it. Here I am quoting Erin E. Devers and Jason D. Runyan, 'The Impact of Thinking Fast and Slow on the Evangelical Mind' (*Christian Scholars Review*, vol. 47, no. 4, 2018), p. 433.

Page 13: To quote the behavioural economist Aner Tal. You can read Tal's little article 'Beware the Truthiness of Charts' in the *Harvard Business Review*. Check it out here: https://hbr.org/2015/11/beware-the-truthiness-of-charts.

Page 14: The simple fact is you can lie with statistics without ever having to falsify the results. The classic in this field is Darrell Huff, *How to Lie with Statistics* (Penguin, Harmondsworth, 1973). To get a good handle on how statistics works, you could try David Spiegelhalter, *The Art of Statistics: Learning from Data* (Pelican, London, 2020).

Page 14: Indeed, if you search hard enough, you can make the most unrelated statistics correlate. The joy of spurious correlations is wonderfully catalogued by Tyler Vigen at his website: https://tylervigen.com/spurious-correlations.

Page 16: The clinical psychologist Seth Kalichman. The quote is from Kalichman's book *Denying AIDS: Conspiracy Theories, Pseudoscience, and Human Tragedy* (Copernicus, New York, 2009), p. 102.

Page 17: As Alan Jacobs says. The quote is from *How to Think*, page 17. Jacobs' book is a little gem. Finish reading this, and then buy it.

2. NO, YOU'RE NOT ENTITLED TO YOUR OPINION

Page 18: 'These people are witnesses to an eternal truth'. The Alec Ryrie quote comes from his book *Unbelievers: An Emotional History of Doubt* (Williams Collins, London, 2019).

Page 19: 'You are not entitled to your opinion. You are only entitled to what you can argue for'. Stokes said this in a 2016 article for *The Conversation.* You can find it here: https://theconversation.com/no-youre-not-entitled-to-your-opinion-9978.

Page 20: 'Facts are, for journalists, the essential ingredient, like flour for bakers or clay for sculptors'. Taylor said this in the middle of the COVID pandemic, in a long essay for *The Guardian*: https://www.theguardian.com/australia-news/2020/sep/06/as-our-former-lives-dissolve-into-uncertainty-facts-are-something-solid-to-cling-to.

Page 21: The way he sees it, nature is both beautiful and brutal. And for him, the facts of science mean there likely is no God. I make this judgement based on comments that Attenborough gave to the Australian interviewer Andrew Denton for a 2003 episode of the show *Enough Rope* (22 September to be exact).

Page 21: Fritz Schaefer, a leading chemist at MIT. You can read Schaefer for yourself with his book *Science and Christianity: Conflict or Coherence?*, 2nd edn (Apollos, Watkinsville, 2013).

Page 22: If you consult books on logic and reasoning. This is hardly going to be your next 'beach read', but maybe you want to check out something like D. Q. McInerny, *Being Logical: A Guide to Good Thinking* (Random House, New York, 2004).

Page 24: Indeed, in one study by Gordon Pennycook. Yes, I know it is just one study. It doesn't prove anything much. But if you want to read it for yourself, see Gordon Pennycook et al., 'Fighting COVID-19 Misinformation on Social Media: Experimental Evidence for a Scalable Accuracy-Nudge Intervention' (*Psychological Science,* vol. 31, no. 7, 2020), pp. 770–80.

Page 24: 'we realized that social influence does not end with the people we know'. This quote comes from *Connected: The Surprising Power of Our Social Networks and How They Shape Our Lives* (Little, Brown and Company, New York, 2009), p. xi.

Page 25: Joey Cheng … posits. You can see the study at Joey T. Cheng et al., 'The Social Transmission of Overconfidence' (*Journal of Experimental Psychology: General*, vol. 150, no. 1, 2021), pp. 157–86.

Page 25: 'When people can publish whatever they want, they do'. This little nugget of goodness from Cullen Murphy can be found in his article 'Before Zuckerberg, Gutenberg' (*The Atlantic*, vol. 325, no. 1, 2020), p. 24.

Page 25: In August 2020, The Guardian *reported*. See https://www.theguardian.com/uk-news/2020/aug/26/shock-an-aw-us-teenager-wrote-huge-slice-of-scots-wikipedia.

Page 28: It reminds me of the story of the old man. The precise origins of this tale are opaque to me. I found the story on Peter Straube's website here: https://eventsforchange.wordpress.com/2011/06/05/the-starfish-story-one-step-towards-changing-the-world/. He, in turn, attributes it to a book by Loren Eiseley called *The Star Thrower*.

Page 28: In the words of Richard Paul. Paul's definition is repeated everywhere in books and websites because it is short, lovely, and insightful. You can find out more here: https://www.criticalthinking.org/pages/critical-thinking-where-to-begin/796.

Page 29: what the philosopher Catherine Hundleby calls 'argument repair'. See https://chundleby.com/2015/01/16/what-is-argument-repair/.

3. PUTTING EXPERTS IN THEIR PLACE

Page 33: 'almost everyone in the class thinks'. Zell's comment is in this BBC News article: https://www.bbc.com/worklife/article/20200923-why-arrogance-is-dangerously-contagious.

Page 34: In 2013, a young woman took to Twitter. This charming anecdote comes from Tom Nichols in his book *The Death of Expertise: The Campaign Against Established Knowledge and Why It Matters* (Oxford University Press, New York, 2017), pp. 83–84. If you want to explore the whole topic of experts in more depth, you want to read Nichols.

Page 34: In 1999 Justin Kruger and David Dunning. The Dunning-Kruger Effect is now a slogan. But if you actually want to read the study that launched the phenomenon, then here it is: Justin Kruger and David Dunning, 'Unskilled and Unaware of It: How Difficulties in Recognizing One's Own Incompetence Lead to Inflated Self-Assessments' (*Journal of Personality and Social Psychology*, vol. 77, no. 6, 1999), pp. 1121–34.

Page 35: 'Higher education is supposed to cure us'. 'Tom Nichols, *The Death of Expertise*, p. 77.

Page 36: 'access to information for their own personal understanding of the information'. This quote comes from Matthew Fisher, Mariel K. Goddu, and Frank C Keil, 'Searching for Explanations: How the Internet Inflates Estimates of Internal Knowledge' (*Journal of Experimental Psychology: General*, vol. 144, no. 3, 2015), p. 674. The Nichols quote is from *The Death of Expertise*, p. 106.

Page 37: Or as the African-American biblical scholar Esau McCaulley puts it. This is based on a tweet made by McCaulley on 13 June 2020. As of this writing, that tweet no longer appears to be available.

Page 37: In 1949, the Portuguese neurologist Antonio Egas Moniz. You can find out more about Moniz by heading to the Nobel Prize website (https://www.nobelprize.org/prizes/medicine/1949/moniz/biographical/) or to this journal article: Siang Yong Tan and Angela Yip, 'António Egas Moniz (1874–1955): Lobotomy Pioneer and Nobel Laureate' (*Singapore Medical Journal*, vol. 55, no. 4, 2014), pp. 175–76.

Page 38: His method of transorbital lobotomy. The gruesome practices of Walter Freeman are detailed in Jessica Matyas, *Famous Case Histories in Neurotrauma* (Routledge, New York, 2021), chapter 7. It's probably not a book to read just before bed, or when you're going in for surgery. The references to a 'surgically induced childhood' and the lady with the 'personality of an oyster' are derived from Mical Raz, *The Lobotomy Letters: The Making of American Psychosurgery* (University of Rochester Press, Rochester, 2013), chapter 5. Again, the cover alone of this book might give you nightmares.

Pages 38–39: To quote Steven Levitt and Stephen Dubner. This quote comes from their book *Think Like a Freak: Secrets of the Rogue Economist* (Penguin, London, 2015).

Pages 39–40: As Nate Silver puts it. This quote from Nate Silver is from his interview with *Fast Company* magazine, available here: https://www.fastcompany.com/3001794/fivethirtyeights-nate-silver-explains-why-we-suck-predictions-and-how-improve.

Page 40: 'The average expert [is] roughly as accurate as a dart-throwing chimpanzee'. See Philip E. Tetlock and Dan Gardner, *Superforecasting: The Art and Science of Prediction* (Random House, London, 2016). To be fair, in that book Tetlock goes on to say that his earlier work has been interpreted too negatively. He was not saying all expert forecasts were useless. Indeed, his more recent work has been devoted to cultivating better approaches to expert prediction. Still, many so-called experts do fail pretty badly.

Page 41: thinking is a 'process, not a conclusion'. Nichols, *The Death of Expertise*, p. 176.

Page 42: 'the cost of saying "I don't know" is higher than the cost of being wrong'. Levitt and Dubner, *Think Like a Freak*, p. 29.

Pages 42–43: 'I seem, then, in just this little thing to be wiser than this man at any rate, that what I do not know I do not think I know either'. Well, at least that's how Plato says Socrates put it. The quote comes from Plato, *Apology* 21c (I'm using the translation from Harold North Fowler).

Page 43: 'A man should never be ashamed to own he has been in the wrong'. This quote from Pope is found on page 836 in Jonathan Swift's *The Works of Jonathan Swift Volume 1*, available at Google Books here: https://www.google.com.au/books/edition/The_Works_of_Jonathan_Swift/sHaZ_T5IZbQC?hl=en&gbpv=0.

Page 43: Tetlock talks of the need to own our mistakes. You can read Tetlock's Ten Commandments of superforecasting here: https://goodjudgment.com/philip-tetlocks-10-commandments-of-superforecasting/.

Page 43: follow the advice of Alan Jacobs. Jacobs, *How to Think*, p. 148.

4. FINDING CONFIDENCE, NOT CERTAINTY

Page 44: 'In the modern world the stupid are cocksure while the intelligent are full of doubt'. Russell said this in a 1933 essay called 'The Triumph of Stupidity'. You can find it in his book *Mortals and Others* (Routledge, London, 2008), p. 204.

Page 44: The human desire for certainty. For a great little summary account of Descartes and his quest for certainty, take half an hour and read Nigel Warburton, *A Little History of Philosophy* (Yale University Press, New Haven, 2011), pp. 62–68.

Page 47: But we would do well to heed the warning of the economist Sarah Hamersma. Hamersma's perceptive comments are found in the article 'Uncertainty: The Beauty and Bedrock of Statistics', available here: https://www.cardus.ca/comment/article/uncertainty-the-beauty-and-bedrock-of-statistics/.

Page 47: As the theologian John Stackhouse defines it. This little quote is taken from his blog 'I'm Certain That There Are Two Kinds of Certainty', which you can view here: http://www.johnstackhouse.com/im-certain-that-there-are-two-kinds-of-certainty/.

Page 48: 'No one exercises "blind faith" in anything or anyone'. This is drawn from Stackhouse's recent book *Can I Believe? Christianity for the Hesitant* (Oxford University Press, Oxford, 2020), p. 18.

Page 51: 'I want atheism to be true'. Thomas Nagel, *The Last Word* (Oxford University Press, Oxford, 1997), p. 130.

Pages 51–52: As the American writer Steven Garber puts it. See https://washingtoninst.org/on-being-implicated/. All of Steven Garber's writing it worth your time, particularly if you are young, or young at heart.

Page 53: Be brave. Jacobs, *How to Think*, p. 148. Seriously, why haven't you bought this book yet? It's a lot better than this one.

5. THE CHARACTER OF A THINKER: HUMILITY, HOSPITALITY, LOVE

Page 54: 'Perhaps you regard this thinking about myself as a waste of time'. This gorgeous quote from Wittgenstein is excerpted from a letter Wittgenstein wrote to Bertrand Russell in 1913. You can read the letter for yourself in Brian McGuinness (ed.), *Wittgenstein in Cambridge: Letters and Documents 1911–1951* (Blackwell, Oxford, 2008), p. 63. Emphasis is in the original.

Page 54: In their book Metaphors We Live By. George Lakoff and Mark Johnson, *Metaphors We Live By* (University of Chicago Press, Chicago, 1980), pp. 4–6. #ShotsFired is my own little addition.

Page 56: As the philosopher Jason Baehr puts it. Jason Baehr, *The Inquiring Mind: On Intellectual Virtues and Virtue Epistemology* (Oxford University Press, Oxford, 2011), p. 2.

Page 57: As the historian Tom Holland says. Tom Holland, *Dominion: The Making of the Western Mind* (Little, Brown, London, 2019), p. 19. Holland writes so well he can make 600 pages of history the perfect summer 'beach read'.

Page 60: The political theologian Luke Bretherton suggests. See Luke Bretherton, *Hospitality as Holiness: Christian Witness Amid Moral Diversity* (Routledge, London, 2010), pp. 121–59.

Page 61: In 2019, the think-tank More in Common. The report is called 'The Perception Gap' and you can digest all its goodness, and even take a diagnostic quiz, here: https://perceptiongap.us/.

Page 61: The French historian Marc Bloch put it well. This quote is taken from Bloch's classic volume *The Historian's Craft* (Manchester University Press, Manchester, 2006), p. 119. It was originally published (in French) in 1949.

Page 61: Steelmanning. Chana Messinger's original blog post is worth a long look. See https://themerelyreal.wordpress.com/2012/12/07/steelmanning/.

Page 62: In the Christian tradition, love is supreme. One could unpack this idea at length. In brief, when Jesus is asked what is the greatest of God's commandments, he says to love God with our whole being and to love others as ourselves (Matthew 22:34–40). The Apostle Paul says that love is the greatest of the virtues (1 Corinthians 13:13). The Apostle John says God is love, and those who know God grow increasingly like him in his love (1 John 4:7–21). I could go on, but you get the point.

CONCLUSION: CONFESSIONS OF AN IMPERFECT FRIEND

Page 64: As my friend and colleague Natasha Moore puts it. These are the closing thoughts from the first book in this series, *The Pleasures of Pessimism* (Acorn Press, Sydney, 2020). It's a cracker of a book.

Page 65: the communications professor Tim Muehlhoff suggested. Muehlhoff has produced many books, articles, and videos on these themes. A good place to start is his video 'How to have a difficult conversation,' available here: https://www.youtube.com/watch?v=az1k3hcGB-4&t=920s.

Page 66: 'The truth can be spoken only by someone who is already at home in it'. This beautiful thought comes from Wittgenstein's *Culture and Value* (University of Chicago Press, Chicago,1980), p. 7.